"I AM A FREE AGENT"

STEVEN K. BURGESS

AND

C. G. COOPER

TABLE OF CONTENTS

Chapter 1: The Change. 5

Chapter 2: A New World 11

Chapter 3: The Free Agent 21

Chapter 4: The Industrial Mindset 36

Chapter 5: Value Add 46

Chapter 6: Who Am I? 55

Chapter 7: New Friends 66

Chapter 8: What Do You Do? 77

Chapter 9: My Life 84

CHAPTER 1
THE CHANGE

I'll never forget. It was a Thursday. Work was crazier than ever, and my wife and I had stayed up late the night before packing for our coming vacation. I was exhausted and it wasn't even noon.

My cell phone buzzed and I looked down. It was my boss.

Stop by my office when you have a minute.

I honestly didn't think about it. Jack made similar requests on a daily basis. As one of his five vice presidents, I was often called in to give the CEO my take on an upcoming marketing campaign, a potential hire, or a quarterly earnings report.

After finishing the email I was writing to one of our best customers, I stood up and yawned with an extended stretch. I remember thinking, *I'll get some sleep when we get to the lodge.* My wife Kathy had booked a four-night stay at a ski resort three hours away. Both kids were in college, so for the first time in a long while, it would be just the two of us.

I'd been promising Kathy a getaway since our youngest left for her freshman semester eight months earlier.

Thoughts of sleeping-in and running the slopes consumed my attention as I walked down the hall to my boss's corner office. Things were hectic and employees rushed around like bees in a hive. I said hello to co-workers as they rushed past.

The first thing I noticed when I walked in Jack's office was the other attendees, Norma, our head of human resources, and Hank, our attorney.

"Hey, guys." I waved with a smile.

"Have a seat, Matt," said Jack, his normally genial face set in a neutral poker stare.

I took a seat, not necessarily concerned, but wary. In my head I assumed the company was being sued or something had gone wrong in one of our many factories. It had happened before and would undoubtedly happen again.

Norma and Hank weren't giving any clues. They sat as stoically as our boss.

"So, what's up?" I asked, hoping to cut the tension that was threatening to bring my mood down.

Jack ran a hand through his wavy dirty blonde hair. "We're making some changes, Matt."

My stomach clenched. The pieces fell into place before he spoke.

"You know what an integral part of the company you've become. That's why it was such a hard decision…"

I don't remember the rest. I'm sure I just sat there with my jaw hanging open. Before I knew it, I'd signed some type of release that Norma slid across Jack's desk. Hank was next with the particulars of my severance package that he said was, "Quite generous."

I nodded stupidly and signed everything they wanted signed. *This can't be happening,* I thought.

So after ten years of helping to build the company that had only been in its infancy when I arrived, they were letting me go. Me, a vice president of one of the fastest growing companies in the city.

By the time I got back to my office, my stuff was already packed neatly into four cardboard boxes and stacked on a dolly handled by one of two security guards.

"We'll escort you out, sir," said Frank, the larger of the two guards and a former college football standout who'd been on the company basketball team with me four years running. He'd never called me sir before. It was always Matt and Frank.

I nodded and followed the dolly toward the exit and out into a new world.

NOTES

NOTES

CHAPTER 2

A NEW WORLD

Driving home as slowly as I dared, I prepared myself for the conversation with Kathy. After giving her an extended hug, I told her what had happened and softened the blow of the unwelcome news by telling my wife about all the time we'd have to spend together in the coming months.

"Are you okay, honey?" she asked, worry etched clearly in her expression.

"I'll be fine. Just a bit of a shock." And it was. I'd been laid off once before, but that had been right out of college in my buddy's start-up. Sure, I'd changed jobs a couple times, but those had always been my choice. I felt like what I imagined a guy going through a divorce would feel. Alone. Scared. Worried about going back on the market. "How about we finish getting packed?"

My wife nodded and left me to my thoughts. What was I going to do?

+++

I put on a brave face and ignored my phone for the first time in years. Instead of waiting to leave in the morning, we took off after our bags zipped closed. It felt good to be on the road. Rather than pester me with questions and concerns, Kathy read a book silently with her tiny feet perched on the dash.

The drive gave me time to get my head together. By then the shock had mostly worn off. Being a man of action, I ran through my options. Headhunters. Friends at other companies. It had been a while since I'd looked for a job, and I realized that things had probably changed.

As soon as we got to the mountain, I'd drop a note to some old buddies who had gone through the job search in recent years. It couldn't be that bad. My resume would need some work, but I was more than qualified. I'd checked as many blocks along the way as I could.

Besides, I could stretch the severance package out for a year if I had to. I was sure it wouldn't take that long. It never had before.

+++

Kathy unpacked her things while I connected to the resort's WiFi. Ten minutes later, I'd sent eight quick emails to my friends letting them know I was back on the job market and would appreciate any suggestions they had. I hadn't talked to any of them in a while. It would be good to catch up and get their opinions.

I clicked the laptop shut and headed off to soak in the hot tub.

+++

Kathy and I ate a late dinner at one of the nicer restaurants on the ski resort grounds. We shared one of every appetizer and talked until the lights went out in the kitchen. It felt like old times.

Walking back to our condo hand-in-hand, Kathy looked up at me. "Is there anything I can do to help with the job search?"

Over dinner I'd outlined my plan. After extending our stay, I'd return home recharged and ready to hit the pavement. I wasn't afraid of hard work.

"Thanks, Kath. I think I'll be okay."

As she got ready for bed I checked my laptop for replies to the messages I'd sent earlier. Five out of the eight had already written back. I perused them quickly, pleased by the general consensus that confirmed my thoughts. There were jobs out there. Each man offered to do anything they could to help. I smiled.

Just as I reached to close the laptop another email pinged my inbox. It was from an old friend from college.

Matt, good to hear from you. Just wanted to let you know that things in the market have changed. If you'd like to chat I'm available most of the day tomorrow. Give me a ring. All the best, Tim

His comment about the market having changed made me pause. None of the others had mentioned it. I knew Tim to be a pretty smart guy, a savvy operator. I jotted down his phone number and headed off to bed, promising myself that I would try to sleep past 7a.m.

+++

After a wonderful brunch and a couple runs down the slopes (the lift was steps from our place), I sat down to call Tim.

He picked up after a couple rings.

"This is Tim."

"Hey, Tim, it's Matt!"

"Hey, partner! How's it going?"

"Not too bad. Me and Kathy are up in the mountains eating too much food and working it off on the slopes. Thanks again for writing me back last night."

"No problem. Sorry it took me a little longer than usual. I had my phone turned off."

"I understand. So, I wanted to ask you about what you mentioned in your email," I said.

"You mean about the market changing?"

"Yeah."

"Look, I don't want to concern you. I'm sure you've got a great resume and a slew of references, but I just went through the same thing last year. When was the last time you had to find a job?"

"Ten years ago," I answered.

"Pretty easy back then?" Tim asked.

"Not painless, but fairly straightforward."

"It sounds like we've been on a similar timeline. The bottom line is that your search may not be as easy as it was in the past. I don't want to scare you, but I do want you to be prepared. Did your old company give you a decent severance?"

"They did."

"Good. Let me tell you what happened to me."

Tim went on to explain that he'd had a similar dismissal from his old company. He and his wife had planned well and budgeted for a year off as the worst case. Six months into his unemployment, Tim still didn't have a job.

"It wasn't for lack of trying," Tim explained. "I mined every contact I'd every made. Three headhunters looked and looked. I kept hearing the same things. They didn't want to pay me the salary I'd made before. I was overqualified, and on and on."

I listened in stunned silence. How does a guy go from making a solid six-figure income to being unneeded?

"What did you end up doing?" I asked, hoping to God that he'd tell me the secret.

Tim chuckled. "If you're looking for a magic spell, I don't have one. Here's what I will do. Let me introduce you to the guy that helped me figure it out. I'll buy the coffee and he can fill you in. I think it'll be an eye-opening conversation for you. It was for me."

"Uh, sure," I stuttered, not liking the turn the conversation had taken with my mind. Fear twisted my stomach and a nervous tingle prickled up my scalp.

"Great. Give me a call when you get home, and I'll set it up."

I thanked Tim for his time and hung up the phone. It couldn't be as bad as he'd said…could it?

PRACTICE

You may be actively looking for a new job or just curious. When was the last time you looked? Do you know what's out there?

Write down the answers to the following questions:

1. When was the last time you looked for a new job?
2. What are your expectations this time around?
3. Who do you know that has recently made a similar move?

4. How long could you support yourself without a job?

5. What would your dream position be?

NOTES

NOTES

_____

_____

_____

_____

_____

_____

_____

_____

_____

_____

_____

_____

_____

_____

_____

_____

_____

_____

_____

_____

_____

_____

CHAPTER 3
THE FREE AGENT

S omehow I was able to keep the nagging doubt at bay for the rest of our vacation. It was wonderful waking up without an alarm and going about however we pleased. I couldn't remember the last time I'd felt so free. Kathy was happier than ever. It was like we were dating again.

A week later, we reluctantly made the trip back home. We took our time, driving on back roads, stopping at as many antique shops as we could. Kathy loved buying hidden gems that she'd later expertly integrate into our home's décor. She had a knack for it.

I went along with a smile and even found an old fishing rod that would look great in my home office.

It was back to reality as soon as we pulled into the driveway. After unloading our luggage, I gathered the collected mail and headed into the house. Sorting through the junk mail, I stopped short. There were two envelopes stacked together, each with my old company's logo stamped on the front.

Holding my breath I opened the first one. It was summary of my extended health benefits. My eyes glazed over after a moment. That could wait. The second envelope held my most recent pay stub. As promised, the amount was larger than normal. Even still, I couldn't bring myself to breathe a sigh of relief. Just the sight of the familiar company marking left me speechless.

"Anything good?" Kathy asked, strolling into the kitchen with an empty suitcase.

"What? Uh, no, not really. Just a bunch of junk."

She didn't comment on my obvious discomfort. Kathy could read me like a book. Instead, she asked, "What would you like for dinner? We're still on vacation." She smiled warmly, and I couldn't help returning it.

"How about I call up that new Thai restaurant? I hear they've got some fantastic green curry," I suggested.

"Sounds good to me. Why don't you have them deliver it? You still owe me a massage," she said with a sly grin.

I nodded and grabbed my cell phone.

+++

The next day, I got to work. My first call was to Tim. We set up a time to meet the following day at a coffee shop a couple miles from my house.

"Bring something to write on," Tim said. "I think you'll want to get it all down."

"Okay. I'll see you tomorrow."

+++

It was a beautiful morning. Not a cloud in the sky. After a jog around the neighborhood and a couple sets of push-ups in the garage, I took a shower and changed for my meeting.

Instead of wearing the suit I was so used to donning for my old job, I threw on a pair of jeans and a sweater Kathy had given me for my birthday. She'd wanted me to wear it, but I'd never had the time.

Inspecting myself in the mirror I deemed that I was appropriately attired for the meet-up. Fifteen minutes later, I pulled into the parking lot of the crowded coffee shop.

I hadn't seen Tim in over two years, but spotted him easily in the crowd. He stood up and greeted me with a smile and handshake.

"Great to see you, Matt."

"You too."

As we took our seats, another man walked up to the table. He was holding three cups of coffee in a hasty triangle between his hands.

"Don't worry about getting up, gentleman," the stranger, who I assumed was Tim's friend, said good-naturedly. "Grab a coffee, and I'll grab a seat."

He was of average height and build. Wearing a well-tailored corduroy sport coat over a t-shirt and jeans, he slid into his chair and took a sip of his coffee.

"You must be, Matt." He offered his hand, which I shook, and said, "I'm Neil."

"Good to meet you, Neil," I replied. "Thanks for taking the time to meet with me."

"I'm happy to do it. Tim tells me that you're on the hunt." Neil's tone was conversational in a way that suggested that he was comfortable speaking in front of large crowds. It wasn't cocky, just self-assured.

"Uh huh. It's been a while since I've had to look," I said.

"What has Tim told you so far?"

"Not much, just that the market has changed and that you helped him out."

Tim grinned. "Sometimes I feel like the word *help* is a major understatement for what Neil did for me. I think a better word might be *saved*."

Neil laughed. "What can I say? You did need saving, right?"

"I sure did," said Tim.

"So Matt, I hope it's okay that Tim shared a bit of your history with me. I also did a little digging online."

"Yeah, no problem. Me and Tim go back a long way."

"Good. Now tell me, how do you categorize your current status?" Neil asked.

"What do you mean?"

"If someone were to ask you what you're doing, what would you say?"

My face must've colored, because I felt the heat rising. I wasn't used to answering those types of questions, and tugged at my collar. "I'm...

well, I guess I would say that I'm temporarily unemployed."

"Okay, so if I'm hearing your right, you're planning on getting a new job?"

"Of course." I started to get a little peeved. Who was this guy? Of course I was looking for another job. What else would I be doing there?

Neil saw my discomfort and raised his hands like a soldier saying he means no harm. "I'm asking because each of us takes a different path. After working with me, Tim decided to rejoin the workforce. How's that working out for you, Tim?"

Tim chuckled. "I'm happier than I've ever been."

"And you're making good money?" Neil asked.

"More than I ever did before."

"So you think the little exercise I put you through last year was worth it?"

"Absolutely," Tim said. "It was eye-opening."

I had no idea what they were jabbering about. Wasn't I supposed to be talking to this guy about finding a job and how best to do it? I can now admit that my ego probably had something to do with it. I wasn't used to casual business. Boardrooms and auditoriums were what I'd experienced for the last fifteen years.

"Are you totally confused yet, Matt?" Neil asked.

"Honestly? Yes. I don't mean to be rude, but what exactly can you help me with?" My patience was sliver thin at that point. I was ready to leave.

Neil and Tim shared a knowing look. Tim spoke first. "It may not feel like it, but you're lucky that the journey begins now. I was way behind when I met Neil."

"He's right," said Neil. "I can only imagine what it must've felt like to be let go."

"It wasn't fun," I admitted.

"It never is. Here's the deal. I'm here to change all that. Now, I'm not a miracle worker, but I can tell you that I've helped a lot of men and women who were in very similar positions."

"Again, I don't mean to be rude, but what's in it for you?" I wasn't used to getting anything for free. There was always a catch.

Neil shrugged. "If you think you'll have to pay me, you won't. I do this for two reasons. First, someone helped me out a few years ago. I like the idea of giving back to God for taking care of me. Second, you can never have enough friends. Some day you and I may do business. You never know. I've come to view the world as a never-ending network that I get to tap into. You may become an integral part of my network."

I relaxed a bit at his explanation. He seemed honest, and yet, I was used to having my guard up. Years of hearing pitches and sales calls had made me naturally skeptical. Networking had never been a necessity. Sure there had been conferences and trade shows, but for the most part other people sought me out, not the other way around.

"What exactly does your approach entail?" I asked cautiously.

"Let's start from the beginning. You said a minute ago that you would classify yourself as unemployed, right?"

"Sure."

"I hate that word, unemployed. It sounds so miserable. The first thing you need to do is shake off that title. If you hadn't noticed, I'm pretty much a glass-is-half-full kinda guy. I like to be optimistic, ready to look on the bright side. What about you? Are you an optimist?"

I thought about it for an extended moment. As I sat there, I realized that no one had ever asked me that question before. I guess it was always assumed that I was a pretty positive guy. I'd smile and chat with most anyone. But

Neil's question made me stop. Maybe it was the lingering shock of being fired. Maybe it was the fear of looking for another job. Maybe it was my ego. Whatever it was, despite my reservations, I answered honestly.

"I guess for the most part, but right now I'm not so sure."

Neil nodded. "I understand. Right now you probably feel like an orphan who just got yanked out of his home. Am I right?"

"Yeah."

"That's completely normal. You're still reeling from an event that's shaken your beliefs. The fix doesn't come over night."

His solemn tone pulled me in. Neil seemed to know the topic well. He waited, knowing I'd ask the question.

"Where do I start?"

"Do you watch football, Matt?"

Football? "Uh, sure, sometimes."

"Good. Are you familiar with how the NFL works these days?" asked Neil.

"I guess."

"What happens when a star quarterback gets traded?"

"He looks for a new team?"

"Yes. How do you think he feels about his prospects? Is he confident in his abilities? Does he think he'll get a new job?"

"If he's a star, yeah," I answered, wondering where the line of questioning was going, hoping he wouldn't grill me on current players. The only time I'd watched football recently was at company Super Bowl parties.

"What do we call a star quarterback who's no longer with a team?"

"A free agent."

"Exactly! A free agent. That's how I want you to feel. You obviously have talent. You're definitely a star. If you do this right you could have the pick of positions out there."

Neil reached into his sport coat and pulled out a small ringed notebook and a pen. Without a word he opened it and wrote something. He tore the sheet out and handed it to me. It said:

> *My Name is (state your name), and*
> *I am a Free Agent*

I looked up. "Okay?"

"Read it out loud with your name where the parentheses are."

"Really?"

"Did you know that the simple act of saying something out loud has the power to make it come true?"

I'd heard similar things from different self-improvement books over the years. "Yeah."

"Have you ever done it?" Neil asked.

"Probably when I was younger."

"Okay. Then it's time to do it again. You need to believe your own worth. Being a free agent means carrying yourself with a certain air of confidence. Think of the star quarterback. Do you think he walks into a prospective team's headquarters with his head hung low? No way! A great quarterback walks in with confidence while remaining humble. He talks about helping the team. He understands that he may have to prove his worth to a new coach and he's okay with that. Being a free agent means understanding your strengths as well as your limitations. Hall of Fame free agents crave a challenge and attack it like a pit bull."

I'd never thought of myself that way before, but Neil's words struck a chord. I knew I was good at what I did. No one would ever call me a loner or not a team player. I could see a lot of correlation between that star quarterback and myself.

"And the first step to becoming that star is for me to read this?"

Neil nodded, smiling peacefully.

I looked around the coffee shop to see if anyone was looking. My neck started to itch. I took a deep breath and said, "My Name is Matt, and I am a Free Agent."

PRACTICE

A Free Agent is someone of value. He or she is a person dedicated to winning no matter the game he plays.

Like Matt, you may be wondering where to go from here. You may have been laid off, underemployed, sick of your job, or just bored. In each and every case, the solution starts with you. It's time to get your mind right. It's time to reboot. It's time to understand your worth.

Read the following out loud, with your name in the middle.

My Name is (state your name), and
I am a Free Agent

You're not finished. Write down your proclamation and keep it handy as you go about your daily routine. Read it out loud when you're getting ready in the morning, when you're in the car, or when you go for a walk. The more times you say it, the more you will believe.

NOTES

NOTES

CHAPTER 4
THE INDUSTRIAL MINDSET

I left that first meeting in a daze. Neil was right. Deep inside, despite my outward calm and confidence, a younger me sat shaking. The scared me didn't know what to do in the new world. Everything had changed since my last foray into the job market.

Driving home, I slid the piece of notebook paper out of my pocket.

My Name is (state your name), and
I am a Free Agent

I read it once in my head, *My Name is Matt, and I am a Free Agent*. Taking a deep breath, I read it aloud, "My name is Matt, and I am a Free Agent."

I said it over an over again, trying to shake the fear, trying to gain the nerve, trying to make the leap. Why was it so hard? Why couldn't I do it?

By the time I pulled into my neighborhood, I was ready to crumple the note and throw it out the window. As I took the last corner and got a glimpse of my house, I caught sight of my wife in the window. She was watering one of the plants hanging in our breakfast nook. My heart ached. I wanted to tell her that I'd found the answer. That's when it happened. Something inside of me popped. I'm not sure if it was my ego or the lock on some long held belief. My mind cleared and I saw the truth. I controlled my destiny. For years I'd lent my freedom to someone else, to my boss, to my company. It was time to regain that control. How had I let it go so far?

Pulling into the garage I looked down at that slip of paper again and read, "My Name is Matt, and I am a Free Agent."

The man that walked in to see his wife was not the same man who'd left earlier in the day. I was now a Free Agent.

+++

After a long talk with Kathy, who, unsurprisingly, liked the change in my attitude, I called Neil and apologized for my less-than-enthusiastic attitude during our meeting.

"Believe it or not, I know what you're going through," Neil replied. "For years you've been conditioned to think a certain way. The system is broken, not you. How about we meet for coffee tomorrow and I'll explain it in more detail."

I readily accepted his invitation and promised to see him the next day. Now that my mind was right, I wanted to move forward. Neil would show me how.

+++

The next day, Neil dove right in. "You're familiar with the industrial revolution?"

"Yes."

"So you know that it started as a way to be more systematic, more efficient. In 1917 the United States wasn't the superpower it is today. Back then, we were struggling to be a top player. Here's what happened. We had plenty of resources, but what we lacked was workers. In order to ramp up production, the captains of industry, prodded by American leadership, had to revamp the system and find a way to create a robust labor pool. What ended up happening was that it changed everything from schooling to outlook.

"Mandatory and standardized public education was instituted not necessarily as a way to make us smarter, but to breed adults that would work in the growing American industries. We went from a country of self-starters and dreamers to a country of worker bees. Over the years the feeling spread and became the norm. You work for a company all your life, and as long as you work hard and keep the boss happy you can retire with a pension."

That was exactly what my father had done. He'd worked for the same company right out of high school up until his retirement.

Neil continued. "Here's the problem. The world changed. The factory jobs that once were the backbone of this country now thrive in other nations around the world. Instead of an industrial economy, we live in a connected economy."

I'd never heard that term. "I think you lost me. What do you mean by *connected*?"

"Do you have any social media accounts?" Neil asked.

"Sure."

"Did you have them twenty years ago?"

"No. The technology hadn't been invented yet."

"Exactly. Technology is the key. Today we can connect with people halfway around the world. We don't have limitations to communication and collaboration like they did in the early nineteen hundreds or even the latter part of the twentieth century."

"What about all the office workers we have in the States?" I asked.

"They're the new factory workers being pushed daily to make new quotas and boost productivity. Those white-collar jobs are the remnants of the industrial revolution. They do what they're told in the hopes of long-term employment, benefits and a decent retirement. But the rules have changed. They're hoping for something that is rare, going on extinct. How long do you think the average length of employment is?"

I had no idea. "I don't know. Ten years?"

"It's actually closer to five. Back in the sixties the average was more like forty years. Do you know why it changed?"

"I'm sure you'll tell me," I said with a grin. Neil had a way of story telling that kept me hanging for the coming punch line.

"If an office worker's only job is to complete every task her boss tells her to do, why can't that boss find someone else?"

I shrugged, seeing his point.

"No one is irreplaceable, including the CEO. Anyone who thinks they can't be replaced is deluding himself."

"So how does it work now? You make it sound like no matter what we do we'll always be fired," I said.

Neil smiled patiently. "The connected economy rewards differently than the industrial economy. Where the industrial economy rewarded workers for conforming and doing what they were told, the connected economy rewards hard workers who come up with new ideas, think outside the box and craft solutions. The connected economy wants change-makers. It rewards connectors."

"What exactly are they connecting?"

Neil laughed. "You name it. People to people, people to products, businesses to businesses, people to businesses. Connection is the name of the game."

"I guess I'm still a little confused. How is that different than before?" I asked.

"In a connected society, those who connect the best get compensated more."

It finally made sense. My squeaky wheels turned.

"You're saying it's pay for performance?" My former employer had floated a hybrid model of the same concept Neil was talking about. Many of the old-timers, myself included, had scoffed at the idea. Looking back, I realized the thought of disturbing my safety net had scared me.

"That's exactly what I'm talking about. If you were running a business, would you rather pay more to have higher producing commissioned salespeople or more worker bees?"

"More sales means more profit, so I guess it's more great salespeople."

"Bingo."

PRACTICE

We now live in a connected economy. There isn't much we can't accomplish with technology. Have you taken a step back to see who you're connected with?

Here's your homework: If you don't have one already, sign up for a LinkedIn account. Don't worry, it's free. Build your profile. If you already have one, clean it up by having a professional photo that shows off your personality, write a good summary detailing your strengths, etc.

The next part is fun. Look for more contacts. LinkedIn's system is super smart and will find friends and old colleagues you'd completely forgotten about. Don't go crazy trying to connect with people you don't know. Stick with those you do.

This is the first step in finding your connecting worth.

NOTES

NOTES

CHAPTER 5
VALUE ADD

Neil continued the lesson, giving an assortment of examples of companies as varied as Apple to Tractor Supply that were using new strategies to find and retain talent.

"Being able to connect isn't the only factor companies are looking for. CEOs are looking for employees that can add value to their company."

"What kind of value do they want us to add?" I asked, jotting down *Value Add* in my small notebook.

"They don't want Yes Men. They want team members who can challenge the status quo, come up with real world solutions and push others to do the same."

That didn't sound so bad. I was a pretty innovative guy. There hadn't been much of a chance to flex my creative muscles in my last job, but I was pretty sure I could handle it.

"What's the catch? It can't be that easy," I said.

Neil smiled. "You're right. Not just the job description has changed, so has the compensation."

My stomach tightened. Money. Of course. I'd dreaded this part of the conversation.

"How has compensation changed?" I asked, already thinking the worst. I'd made a solid six-figure income. Was Neil about to tell me something that would shatter my lifestyle?

"It's like you said before, pay for performance. Fewer companies are paying large salaries. The model is more along the lines of a base plus commission or profit sharing. It's a more sustainable pay structure."

My insides de-knotted. That didn't sound too bad. It would be a first for me, but the chance to make more money might be fun.

"Can you give me an example?"

Neil nodded. "Let's say a woman that used to be a top exec at a company made two hundred thousand dollars per year in salary. Now, with the way things have changed, a new company might look to pay one hundred thousand in base salary and give her the ability to make two fifty or three hundred through incentives."

My gut tightened again. That was a big cut. I'd never worked on commission or profit sharing. I'd had bonuses in the past, but those had been at the sole discretion of the president of the company.

"Wow. I hadn't realized things had changed so much. Is it like that everywhere?"

"Most companies have shifted, especially with their executive positions, into a value add system. If you think about it, it makes sense. Be a superstar and you'll get paid for it. Fail to deliver and you're sent packing. It's smart business, Matt."

I couldn't disagree. There'd been more than a few subpar execs I'd worked with over the years. Luckily most of them had seen the writing on the wall and left before getting the boot. I wondered if I'd fallen into the same bucket of mediocrity. Neil read my mind.

"Before you start questioning your performance, realize that there are still plenty of companies making the shift to the newer model. Yours may have been one of them. They're left with a couple options, change everything over or keep pay where they have it. Your employer might've been one that realizes starting from scratch was easier. Again, that's business."

I should've seen the writing on the wall. For close to a year the company had been making changes, getting leaner, experimenting with new processes. Sitting at that coffee table I realized that I'd gotten complacent. The comfort of having a job had dulled my senses. I didn't want to be a relic. I wanted to be part of the solution.

"How do I take that information and find a new job?"

"The first step is understanding the new system. I've mentored numerous men and women who, before I got a hold of them, went into interviews with huge chips on their shoulders. They walked out thoroughly miffed when they weren't shown the respect they thought they deserved or served a compensation plan they hadn't expected. It's a tough lesson to learn if you don't know what you're getting into."

He was right. I tried to image how it would've gone if I'd met with a prospective employer and they'd offered me a big cut in my base pay. Embarrassingly enough, I can say that I probably would've been like the people Neil had mentioned, whose egos didn't get it.

"That's where the free agent thing comes in, right?" I said.

Neil grinned. "You got it. Just like the star quarterback we talked about, you have to be a team player ready to be challenged, a visionary ready to tackle the future.

I started to see the possibilities. In the past, I'd resented not being compensated for my time and effort. Why did I get paid as much as the joker down the hall that took two-hour lunches and had the leadership potential of a spoiled child? The thought of making decisions that really mattered struck a chord of longing deep inside. By being static, I'd given up the ability to change. There'd been plenty of work to do, but what was it all for?

Neil interrupted my introspection. "Another thing that's changing is resumes. Gone are the days of padded portfolios. More companies want to know you; they want to experience who Matt really is. Some will do this through an extended interview schedule, a personality profile test or maybe a working interview where you're brought in to collaborate with part of their team. Employers are getting smart. They'd rather spend extra time on the front end to get the right fit."

Part of me liked the sound of what Neil was saying, but the old-timer in me fidgeted. I was used to a world where a resume was a listing of accomplishments, essentially checks in the block. It was easier to compare apples to apples that way. The new process Neil described felt more genuine with a strategy behind it. I felt myself warming to the idea.

I asked, "How do I prepare for that kind of interview process?"

"Over the next week, I want you to write down each value you bring to a prospective employer. In addition, I want you to think about how a new business, possibly one you start yourself, would benefit from your involvement. Remember, it's not just the skills everyone puts on their crummy resumes, it's intangibles, life skills, personality traits."

PRACTICE

Write down what "value" you bring to a new company. Stay away from mundane skill descriptions like Spreadsheet Specialist, PowerPoint Expert and Typist of 1,000 words per minute. Stick to what makes you unique.

See if any of these questions help:

- What terms describe your character?

- What types of projects do you like to work on?
- How do you judge a person's character?
- How do you motivate others?
- Do you have 1,400 connections on LinkedIn?
- Do you have 50,000 followers on a given social media platform?
- Do you have a blog?
- Have you been published?

NOTES

NOTES

CHAPTER 6
WHO AM I?

For the next two days I tried to ignore everything I thought I knew about getting a job. Instead, I focused on the homework Neil had given me.

The exercise took some getting used to, and I was finally able to break my writer's block with help from my wife. After explaining what I was doing, Kathy rattled off a stream of examples of values I would bring to an employer.

I smiled as she finished.

"What?" she asked, thinking I was mocking her.

"You know me pretty well, lady."

Kathy stepped closer and put her arms around me. "I've always been proud of you, honey. For a long time I thought you were selling yourself short. I know you can do much more than you might think."

Holding her at arm's length, I stared at her in wonder. How was it that my wife had that much confidence in my abilities?

"Thanks, Kath."

After another hug, she left me to my work. It was a lot easier after that. My wife's words were a revelation. I'd gotten so used to thinking of myself in skill sets that I'd glossed over tallying my own intangible characteristics.

I grinned like kid in a candy store as I typed away.

+++

A week after our previous meeting, I met Neil at the same coffee shop. I made sure to get there early so I could buy his coffee. Seriously, it was the very least I could do. I hoped to do more in the future.

Neil strolled in with his usual t-shirt and sport coat. The shirt simply said *BOOM*. I pointed to the word questioningly as he walked up.

Neil shrugged. "I think today's gonna be a great day. I've already had more than one mind explosion this morning. Thought the shirt was appropriate."

"*Mind explosion?*" I asked.

"You know, when you have a breakthrough, get past something you've been struggling with?"

I chuckled. Neil was teaching me new ways of looking at a lot of things. *Mind explosion* did sound more exciting than an epiphany.

Neil grabbed his coffee with a nod and asked, "How did your assignment go?"

I told him, including the part about Kathy helping me get started.

"I don't know what I'd do without my wife. Mary's been there through the ups and the downs. Her understanding of my mood and needs never ceases to amaze me."

"Yeah. Kathy's the same way."

"Here's to great wives." Neil offered up his coffee cup and we toasted our wives with a muted knock.

"What are we talking about this time?" I asked, eager to further my transition.

"It's all about you."

"Me?"

"Yes," said Neil. "Who are you, Matt?"

"I don't know what you mean," I answered, trying to understand what Neil was saying.

"You are no longer Matt the Vice President. Who are you?"

I considered the question. Neil wasn't being confrontational; he had a point somewhere in his pressing. "I'm a free agent," I said, as confidently as I could.

"We know that. What I'm asking is who are you as a person? How do others identify with you? Who is Matt? Let me give you an example. Five years ago, I left the company I was working for at the time. There were a variety of factors that went into my decision, but mostly I just wasn't happy. I had some money put away and with it Mary and I hit the road. We rented an RV and drove until we saw something interesting. Then we stopped and stayed as long as we wanted. That went on for four months. In that time, away from all the commotion of the world, three things happened. First, I got closer to my wife. I can't tell you how much that time meant to both of us. We still talk about it and pull out the big photo album we put together when we got back. Second, it gave me time to decompress. Getting away and getting out of your own head is so important. You never realized how much garbage accumulates in your mind. It took me weeks just to learn to relax. Third, I found out who I was. It didn't happen overnight, but it happened. When it did, everything changed."

I hadn't realized that I'd leaned forward more and more as he was talking. It was the first time Neil had described his own journey. "What did you find out?" I asked.

Neil laughed. "It was at one of those cheesy fireworks stops along the highway where the mind explosion happened. Mary was buying a drink or something and I walked the aisles reliving memories from my youth of Roman candle battles and bottle rocket cannons. My subconscious drifted to my days mowing lawns, selling gum at school to my friends, walking dogs for neighbors... The nostalgia and feeling of happiness flooded my senses. That's when I knew I could never work for anyone ever again."

It took me a second to get what he was saying. "Wait, you're saying you didn't go back and look for a job?"

Neil shook his head. "I've always been a pretty disciplined person when I'm left on my own. The only job I could remember that I'd actually enjoyed was an internship during college where the young CEO had given me free reign to do research into the company's target market. For me it was a mission. He never once looked over my shoulder. Instead, he gave me a deadline and told me to present my findings to his board of directors. Do you know what that kind of responsibility does for a twenty-one-year-old? Well, I took those two weeks and worked my tail off. I looked in places others hadn't thought of looking. By the time the board meeting happened, I'd identified two new markets I thought the company should expand into and one they should no longer target. I'll never forget the looks on the board members' faces. While the CEO sat with a smile, the others sat in shocked silence. I could see the terror in their eyes and the unspoken question: 'Why did the boss let this *kid* do this?' I didn't know it at the time, but the CEO was new and one of his assignments from the shareholders was to modernize the company. I was part of that process. The CEO was essentially saying, 'If a college kid can think outside the box, why can't we?' I'll never forget that man."

"What happened after that? Did they offer you a job?"

"I was still in college for another year so they couldn't do much with me. Before I graduated, I touched base with the CEO. He'd given me his direct line, and he did offer me a position. Unfortunately, I told my parents about it, including the benefits package, which was eerily similar to what we're seeing these days, twenty-some years later…"

"Base plus commissions," I said.

"Yes. Well, my parents wanted me to get something more stable, and frankly, my mind wasn't where it is today. I thanked the CEO for his offer and declined the invitation."

"Do you regret not saying yes?"

"Nope."

"Why not?"

"Matt, I don't regret any of the lessons I've learned along the way. If I hadn't won, lost, excelled, screwed up and failed I would not be the man I am today. It took me walking that road to live the life I now live. I would not be a successful entrepreneur without the benefit of my experiences."

Slowly I was pealing away layer upon layer of my new friend. I couldn't remember ever meeting anyone who was so humble and open about his failures and rejections. It was refreshing to sit with a person who completely knew who he was.

"How do I find that?" I asked.

Neil smiled. "Get out there and live. Take the time and figure out what you like to do. What are the hobbies you've neglected because of a job? Who have you forgotten about that you might want to see again? Through those interactions and experiences you'll find out who you are. Remember, my clarity came in the middle of a Podunk fireworks shop. You never know when or where it'll happen."

The way Neil told the story made the end goal that much more appealing. I'd have to do some serious thinking. One thought blared in my brain: *Who am I?*

PRACTICE

Who are you? Are you an entrepreneur? Are you a great mother? Are you a preacher?

We all have different paths to take. No two people are identical. You are unique.

Take the time to explore your likes and dislikes. Here are some activities that could help you find out who you are:

-   Take up a new/old hobby.

- Spend time with a friend you haven't seen in a few years.
- Sit and think.
- Write down ten things you're passionate about.
- Write about how you feel about the future.
- Go on a vacation.
- Describe how you envision yourself in ten years.
- Spend time with your significant other.
- Go on a date.
- Pray.
- Eat new foods.
- Go for a walk.

NOTES

NOTES

CHAPTER 7
NEW FRIENDS

Neil and I didn't meet again for another two weeks. During that time, Kathy and I went on another vacation. She knew I used to love fishing, so we rented a small vacation house that sat on a secluded lake. I spent my mornings fishing and thinking. By the time I came in for lunch, Kathy had a spread waiting. We'd take our time and just talk. Some days we'd take a nap, and others we'd go for a walk. We'd given our kids the home phone number in case of an emergency and turned our cell phones off.

I hadn't been without my phone in years. For the first three days I constantly patted my pocket to see if it was there. Weird, huh? I had no idea how attached I was to that thing.

+++

I hadn't had a 'mind explosion' as Neil called it, but I returned refreshed. Never in our nearly thirty years of marriage had we spent close to two weeks away from home.

Neil was waiting with two others when I entered the coffee shop at the appointed hour. I'd slept in and had just barely made it on time. Neil stood up from the table as I approached.

"You look more at ease than I've seen you, Matt."

I grinned, shook Neil's hand and simply said, "Kathy and I had a great trip."

Neil nodded knowingly. "Let me introduce you to a couple of friends. To my left, in the tailored suit, is Carrie."

Carrie stood and shook my hand. She stood close to six feet tall and had striking sapphire eyes. "Nice to meet you, Matt. You're in good hands with Neil."

"And this squidgy gentleman to my right in the workout gear is Kent."

Kent reached a hand across the table. "I hope you haven't taken Neil too seriously, Matt," Kent said, one eyebrow raised humorously. "You know he used to be a snake oil salesman, right?"

I laughed with the others and took a seat. Neil had coffee waiting for me that I grabbed eagerly. I was still on vacation time and needed the pick-me-up.

"I wanted you to meet two others who've gone through similar experiences as you," said Neil. "They both agreed to tell their stories and answer any questions you have. Sound good?"

"That would be great," I answered, dying to hear from Neil's friends.

"Carrie, ladies first. Why don't you tell Matt where you were when we met and what you're doing now," said Neil.

Carrie wiped a smidge of latte from the corner of her mouth and began her tale, "As was my plan, I went to college, continued on to law school and got a job as an associate in an environmental law firm in Los Angeles. I'd interned with them for two summers and believed the fit would work. I really thought I'd be there for years. The internships had been fun and educational. The reality of working at the firm turned out to be something else completely. From day one they tasked me out to partners to do all their research and grunt work. I'm surprised I didn't have a nervous breakdown my first month. Things got better as I learned the routine and my hard work started paying off. A couple cases were thrown my way and I was beginning to feel like part of the team instead of just another cog in the grind. Not long after my second year there, a competitor purchased the firm and we merged offices. It was hectic, but I enjoyed meeting the new associates. As soon as everything was moved into my new office, which I shared with two other young attorneys, we were all called into the large boardroom. Our senior partner had an announcement. In a nutshell, he told us that during the next six months we would all, partners included, be evaluated on our performance. It turned out that performance meant hours billed. All of a sudden there was a mad rush to bill more hours, do more work. My sixty-hour weeks turned into ninety-hour weeks.

"Fast forward to Christmas of that year, which was three months into our evaluation period, and I'd come home to visit my parents. On the way in I stopped at this very coffee shop to double up on my caffeine. In those days I started my mornings with at least two espressos. I must've looked awful because my parents peppered me with questions about my job, was I eating, how were my hours, et cetera. I'd finally had enough and left the house. I was embarrassed and frightened. I didn't want to admit to my parents, and my father especially, who owned his own law firm, that I was drowning. My dad chased after me and we had some heated words. After I calmed down, he asked me how I was feeling. That's when I lost it and broke down. I cried all the way home propped up against my poor father.

"I slept for almost two days, and when I woke up my parents were waiting. Together they told me that they would support me in anything I chose to do, but were concerned for my health and well-being. I opened up and told them about the company merger, the new hours, the demands and my complete lack of a personal life. To their credit, they sat and listened patiently. After I talked for what was probably an hour, my dad said, 'I think there's someone you should meet.' The next day he introduced me to Neil."

"I know Carrie won't mind me saying this, but she was kind of a mess," said Neil. "I'll never forget those hollow eyes." Neil shook his head as if trying to will the thought away. "Carrie was resistant at first, but came around once I told her how I could help."

Carrie patted Neil on the arm the way old friends do. "It was almost an intervention." Carrie smiled. "For the week I was home, Neil came by every day and helped me analyze my life. We were on kind of a time crunch since I had to get back to L.A., but I walked away with a game plan."

I was curious to see what this obviously bright young woman had done. "What happened?" I asked.

"I went back to L.A. and gave my two-weeks notice. No one batted an eye. Before, I would've taken that as a bad sign, but in that moment I realized what I wanted: an employer who cared about my well-being and who I was happy to work for. I moved back home and took my old room. Mom and Dad were super supportive. They told me to take my time, and I did. Neil helped me figure out who I was. I jumped into interviews with a newfound supply of energy and courage. Long story short, I went to work with my dad. He offered to make me a partner of his small firm and I got to work on the cases I wanted. Dad showed me how to grow my client base. Within a year we'd opened a new division at the firm and it's now my responsibility. Dad will probably never retire, and that's okay. He's letting me run more and more of the company, and I can honestly say that I love working with him."

"You don't regret it?" It seemed like a huge leap of faith to me.

"Not one bit. I have my life back and how much money I make is entirely up to me. Never in a million years would I have thought about being an entrepreneur, but that's what I've become. Oh, and I'm engaged."

Neil and Kent spoke up at the same time.

"You didn't tell us!" said Kent.

"Congratulations!" exclaimed Neil.

There were hugs and smiles as the friends enjoyed Carrie's announcement. I sat there feeling happy for Carrie, but a twinge of jealousy crawled up my chest. Wishing I'd found the same clarity years before, I focused on savoring the moment and soaking up the happiness of three people who'd found the lives they were meant to lead.

Finally, the commotion died down and Neil pointed to Kent. "You're up."

Kent nodded. "My story isn't quite as dramatic as Carrie's. I was a typical corporate guy. I have a background in marketing and design. Someone figured out that I was good with people, so before I turned thirty I was already managing a large division. Fast-forward ten years, and I'm bored out of my mind. Sure, there were challenges, but I was stuck. I noticed my work slipping and I decided to do something about it. My boss let me take a full month off, mostly because I had so much vacation time stocked up. I'd always been pretty smart with my money, so I decided to start in Maine, rent a car, drive down the east coast and stop and surf whenever I wanted. When I hit Key West, I hopped on a flight to San Diego and did the same thing going north on the West Coast.

"It was amazing. I'd never felt so alive. I met new friends in the most unlikely places. Along the way I started writing. By the time I got home, I had half of a novel written. Then came the hard part. I could either go back to work or explore life a bit more. Thanks to my excess leave time, I extended my time off by two weeks. During that time I met Neil and you probably know what happened next."

"What do you do now?" I asked, yearning to feel the same way he felt.

"Neil introduced me to some friends along the way. One of them was looking to start a new company here in town. We talked at length one night over dinner and hit it off immediately. Turns out that he needed a marketing guy. A week later I left my old company and helped start a new one. Oh, and I still write and publish novels in my free time."

I shook my head in wonder.

"Sounds crazy, huh?" Neil asked.

"Not really," I said. "I'm just impressed. You all had the courage to go into the unknown. I'm not sure if I'm necessarily there yet, but I sure am encouraged by what you've told me." I really was. Never in my life had I met people like these. I'd been in a corporate cocoon for too long.

PRACTICE

Reach out to ten people you know who've recently (within the last two years) been through a professional transition (you can easily access this information on LinkedIn). Ask them if they wouldn't mind walking you through their story over a cup of coffee.

Don't forget to see if they'll introduce you to friends who may have also transitioned in the last two years.

NOTES

NOTES

CHAPTER 8
WHAT DO YOU DO?

Hearing Carrie and Kent's story motivated me to start looking. I promised myself that I would not limit the search to traditional jobs. After his friends had left, Neil gave me some pointers on where to look and offered to introduce me to his contacts as needed.

I stared dumbfounded as a thought struck me like a throat punch. "Wait, I can't believe I've never asked you this, but can you tell me more about what you do for a living?"

Neil laughed at what must have been a ridiculously silly look on my face. "Don't worry about it. Like I told you before, this process is for you."

"Will you still tell me what you do? I really want to know." And I did. I couldn't fathom my self-centeredness. How had this man helped me for weeks and I'd never thought to reciprocate in any way other than to buy him coffee? I filed the lesson away.

"Of course I'll tell you. Where to start? You already know I left my old company five years ago and my wife and I went on our little road trip. Coming back, I knew I couldn't work for anyone else. Initially I got some small consulting gigs that turned into larger short-term jobs. I honestly didn't like the industry so I took a friend's advice and started looking around. I'd always loved helping people, and with the lessons I'd learned on the road and in my past life, I began pairing transitioning professionals with companies looking for employees."

"You were a headhunter?"

"I prefer the title *talent scout*." Neil smiled. "I still do that occasionally, but about two years out of corporate America I was introduced to three things that would change my life forever: entrepreneurship, residual income and network marketing."

I was glad Neil hadn't mentioned this earlier. Especially at the words 'network marketing' the old me would've jumped in the car and never come back. The new me was ready to learn about how the world worked. If it hadn't been for the lessons I'd learned from Neil, I never would have been so open-minded.

"How did those things help you?" I asked.

"Well, first I learned how to start a business. It was better to do my consulting and talent scouting under the umbrella of a business structure. Then, I found out about the magic of residual income, or what some people call recurring monthly revenue. I loved the idea of doing something once and getting paid for it over and over. It was my friend, who happens to be a writer, who told me about it. After that, I scoured the Internet for residual income opportunities. I wasn't a musician or a writer, so the next fit was network marketing. I reached out to a couple of friends who I knew were involved with different network marketing companies and they gave me the rundown. Knowing that I wanted to stay in the 'professional' world without having to be corporate, I narrowed down the companies to the ones that would fit into my brand. I've never looked back."

"So you're actually running a couple different businesses?"

Neil nodded. "Three to be exact. One is for consulting, the second is for finding talent, and the third is my network marketing organization.

I make more money now than I ever did in a traditional job, and I get to do business with the people and companies I want. It's not for everyone, but it's a perfect fit for me. I make my day. My success is based on my efforts and not the whims of shareholders or corporate bigwigs."

It made perfect sense for Neil. He always looked at peace, like a guy who's found his calling. I wanted that.

"Do you think I might be able to do something similar?" I asked, wanting the same contented freedom Neil had.

"Maybe. That's your journey to take. I'm here to help guide your quest."

Neil gave me a couple resources to check out online and promised to get me in touch with anyone in his sphere of influence. I left the coffee shop buzzing with adrenaline. I was ready.

PRACTICE

Have you considered a life outside the traditional establishment? The new connected economy rewards professionals who bring value to the equation.

Now it's your turn. Evaluate the three things Neil mentioned: entrepreneurship, residual income and network marketing.

Entrepreneurship: Starting and running a business isn't for everyone, but it may be a perfect fit for you. Visit www.Inc.com, www. Entrepreneur.com and www.FastCompany.com. Read about the businesses they profile every month and the people that run them.

Residual Income: Does the idea of doing work once and getting paid over and over excite you? We're talking about legitimate opportunities where you have to put in the time and effort to see results. Sound appealing?

Network Marketing: Opinions vary widely when it comes to network marketing. Read reviews online and you'll see, just like in any other business, the good, the bad and the ugly. The truth of the matter is that network marketing allows highly focused individuals to build a business and a life to be proud of. Network marketing rewards professionals who subscribe to the connected economy. Could it be a good fit for you?

NOTES

NOTES

CHAPTER 9
MY LIFE

Over the next couple months, I explored and evaluated my options. While Neil's life seemed preferable, I wanted to keep as many doors open as I could. I went on interviews and sat in coffee shops. I reached out to friends I hadn't talked to in ages. Kathy got involved and started a 'Good and Bad' chart that we kept stuck to the front of the fridge. On the chart I wrote the things I did and did not want to do for the rest of my life. I remember the day I said I did not want to sit behind a desk. It may seem trivial, but it was a revelation for me.

Under 'Good' went things like being outdoors, networking, paid for my efforts, date nights, fishing, residual income, and having lunch with friends. Under 'Bad' I wrote things like board meetings, coat and tie, travel without Kathy, and a crappy boss.

The list grew longer and longer as my search progressed. One day Kathy mentioned how unlike the old me the 'Good' side of my list looked. I'd had the same realization. How had I lived such an unfulfilling life?

Neil did as promised, and guided me along the way. He was always available to answer questions or point me to someone or something that could. We became great friends, and he had Kathy and me over for dinner where his wife Mary cooked the most amazing lasagna I've ever had.

Kathy saw the benefits of our new life as well. She knew I'd have to go back and do something, but she even offered to start looking for a job herself if we had a hard time making ends meet. We weren't to that point yet, but I appreciated her willingness to help.

+++

It's been eight months since I was fired from my old company. I haven't gone back to the corporate world. With Neil's help, I've done some consulting, but I don't think I'll ever jump back in full-time. Now that I have the attitude of a free agent, I understand my worth. I know the value I add. I get paid for my efforts. Kathy likes it because we still get to do a lot of the things together. It doesn't hurt that I get paid way more for my time than I used to.

I'd looked into the network marketing thing, but nothing jumped out at me. A funny thing happened the other day. I mentioned that I've re-connected with old friends and colleagues, working to flex my newfound connector muscles. It's been fun and beneficial.

Like I was saying, a couple days ago I found an old co-worker from my last company. It's amazing who you can find online! Long story short, he was a friend and we competed for similar positions for years. Three years before my departure, Rick left the company. I'm ashamed to say that I was so relieved that my competition had whittled down that I never reached out after his little farewell party in the company lounge.

He was happy to get my message and suggested Kathy and I come over for lunch the next day. Kathy, who used to spend considerable time with Rick's wife Patricia, agreed immediately. "It'll be wonderful to see them again," she said.

The next day, we pulled up to Rick's beautiful, and large, home in a private golf community.

Kathy's eyes took it all in, obviously impressed by the spread. Rick and Patricia walked out a second later and met us with handshakes and hugs.

Our wives split off for the kitchen and Rick took me for a quick tour. All I could do was nod. Rick never once bragged. You could tell he was proud of the home they'd built, but it was more of a quiet pride like you have for your kids.

When we finally stepped out onto the back patio overlooking the golf course, I closed my eyes and took a deep breath in. "I've gotta ask, Rick, how did you do it? Where did you go after you left the company?"

Rick smiled and offered me a cushy lounger. We sat and he explained, "Three years before I left, Patricia started a little business with a network marketing company. I was not on board at first. I was too busy. You remember those days."

I did. There'd been a running joke at work about who would rack up the most overtime if the company actually paid us overtime. In fact, now that I think about it, it was Rick who'd come up with the game.

"Well, Patricia was pretty motivated. She secretly wanted me to, at some point, quit my job and run the business with her. I think the fact that we were in our mid-forties, without kids, really put things in perspective for her. My realization came a year later. No one at work knew about it, but I had a minor heart attack and had to take medical leave. Patricia was right there with me through it all. I gotta tell ya, I'm a pretty tough guy, but that episode scared me to death. I looked around wondering why I was doing it all. The most important person in my life wanted me home and all I did was work, thinking that it would provide us with the perfect life. Stupid, really." Rick shook his head sadly, and then looked up, a smile warming his face. "That heart attack was the best thing that ever happened to me. It made me realize what I really wanted."

"What did you want?" I asked.

"I wanted to live the way I wanted to live. I didn't want others telling me how to run my life. The need for freedom pulled me irresistibly. My vision cleared. I pulled back a bit from work and helped Patricia build our network marketing business. I was amazed at what she'd done without me, and she was so humble about it. It made my job a lot easier. She'd been waiting and I ran to her with open arms. Two years later we were making enough for me to leave my job. We've only grown it from there."

Tears welled in my eyes as I sat holding my breath. "I...I..." I stuttered.

"Ask me anything you want." Rick patted my arm as Patricia and Kathy walked out with trays holding our lunch. All I could do was stare in wonder as these two old friends sat next to each other, obviously still deeply in love, and told us story after story about their travels and their ever-growing network around the world.

+++

Darkness had settled by the time we finally left. Kathy grabbed my hand as I pulled out of the long drive. "Are you okay, honey? You didn't say much after lunch."

I didn't know what to say, so instead of talking, I pulled the car over and put it in park. When I could will myself to look at my wonderful wife, tears streamed down my face. Kathy's eyes went wide with fright. "What is it?" she whispered.

I reached out my hand and touched her hair. "I...I know what I want."

"What do you want?"

The words spilled out of my mouth as quickly as the salty tears. "I want what Rick and Patricia have. I want to be with you. I want to build a new life with you. I don't care if we have to cut back. I don't care if we have to make sacrifices. As long as I'm doing this with you, I don't care about anything else."

She sat open-mouthed until a huge smile spread, followed by her own tears. "I want the same thing, Matt. Oh, honey, I love you so much." We held each other and sobbed.

When our emotions finally subsided, I held my wife's hand and drove home. Kathy told me about the conversation she'd had with Patricia, who'd told her all about how she'd waited patiently for Rick to come around. She told me how she'd silently said a prayer that the same thing would happen with us. It did. We spent the rest of the night making plans for the future, for our new life.

+++

I can't believe that was less than a week ago. Since then, we've met with Rick and Patricia again. They were ecstatic, not because we wanted to go into business with them, but because we had a clear vision of our future as husband and wife. We know what we want.

I'm excited for the future. I understand my worth as a free agent. Kathy and I are free agents together. We're free to do what we want. She brings the openhearted enthusiasm and I bring the drive and passion. We're in this together. We're figuring it out as we go.

Well, Kathy's calling, so I better get going. She's got some plans to talk about. I love hearing her eagerness. It's hard to explain unless you're in my shoes. I hope you will be soon.

Don't ever forget your worth to the world. You are unique. You have value. You have the ability to live the life you want in the way you want. Don't let anyone tell you differently. Find your place in the new connected economy, and remember, you are a free agent, unhindered and able to tackle life with both hands. I pray that you grab that potential and run with it.

+++++

NOTES

NOTES

We hope you've enjoyed Matt's story.
If you did, please leave a review on Amazon.

If you'd like more information about
working with author Steven K. Burgess,
please connect with him on LinkedIn:
http://www.linkedin.com/in/stevenkburgess

To see more books in this series and to
subscribe to our **New Release Updates**,
please visit www.TheMentorCode.com

To connect with author C. G. Cooper,
please visit www.CarlosCooper.com

www.ingramcontent.com/pod-product-compliance
Lightning Source LLC
Chambersburg PA
CBHW021411170526
45164CB00002B/604